~A BINGO BOOK~

Kentucky
Bingo Book

COMPLETE BINGO GAME IN A BOOK

Written By Rebecca Stark

ISBN 978-0-87386-510-4

Educational Books 'n' Bingo

Printed in the U.S.A.

DIRECTIONS

INCLUDED:

List of Terms

Templates for Additional Terms and Clues

2 Clues per Term

30 Unique Bingo Sheets (To cut out or copy)

Sheet of Markers (to copy and distribute)

1. **Either cut apart the book or make copies of ALL the sheets. You might want to make an extra copy of the clue sheets to use for introduction and review. Keep the sheets in an envelope for easy reuse.**

2. Cut apart the call sheets with terms and clues.

3. Pass out one bingo sheet per student. There are enough unique sheets for a class of 30.

4. Pass out the markers. You may cut apart the markers included in this book or use any other small items of your choice. Students can also mark the sheets themselves; recopy the sheets as needed for additional games.

5. Decide whether or not you will require the entire sheet to be filled. Requiring the entire sheet to be filled provides a better review. However, if you have a short time to fill, you may prefer to have them do the just the border or some other format. Tell the class before you begin what is required.

6. There are 50 terms. Read the list before you begin. If there are any terms that have not been covered in class, you may want to read to the students the term and clues before you begin.

7. There is a blank space in the middle of each sheet. You can instruct the students to use it as a free space or you can write in answers to cover terms not included. Of course, in this case you would create your own clues. (Templates provided.)

8. Shuffle the sheets and place them in a pile. Two or three clues are provided for each term. If you plan to play the game with the same group more than once, you might want to choose a different clue for each game. If not, you may choose to use more than one clue.

9. Be sure to keep the sheets you have used for the present game in a separate pile. When a student calls, "Bingo," he or she will have to verify that the correct answers are on his or her sheet AND that the markers were placed in response to the proper questions. Pull out the sheets that are on the student's sheet keeping them in the order they were used in the game. Read each clue as it was given and ask the student to identify the correct answer from his or her sheet.

10. If the student has the correct answers on the sheet AND has shown that they were marked in response to the *correct questions,* then that student is the winner and the game is over. If the student does not have the correct answers on the sheet OR he or she marked the answers in response to *the wrong questions,* then the game continues until there is a proper winner.

11. If you want to play again, reshuffle the sheets and begin again.

Have fun

TERMS INCLUDED

Muhammad Ali

Appalachia

Arboretum

Black Mountain

Bluegrass

Daniel Boone

Bordered

Cardinal

Christopher Carson

Civil War

Climate

Coal

Commonwealth

County (-ies)

Covered Bridge(s)

Crop(s)

Cumberland Gap

Cumberland Plateau

Cumberland River

Jefferson Davis

Dulcimer

Eastern Coal Field

Executive Branch

Flag

Frankfort

Goldenrod

Hatfield–McCoy

Honeybee

Industry

Jackson Purchase

Judicial Branch

Kentucky Derby

Kentucky Lake

Legislative Branch

Lexington

Abraham Lincoln

Livestock

Louisville

Mammoth Cave

Motto

Carrie Nation

Native American(s)

Ohio River

Pearl(s)

Pennyroyal

Seal

Song

Union

Western Coal Field

Wilderness Road

Additional Terms

Choose as many additional terms as you would like and write them in the squares. Repeat each as desired.
Cut out the squares and randomly distribute them to the class.
Instruct the students to place their square on the center space of their card.

Kentucky Bingo

Clues for Additional Terms

Write three clues for each of your additional terms.

_____ 1. 2. 3.	_____ 1. 2. 3.
_____ 1. 2. 3.	_____ 1. 2. 3.
_____ 1. 2. 3.	_____ 1. 2. 3.

Kentucky Bingo

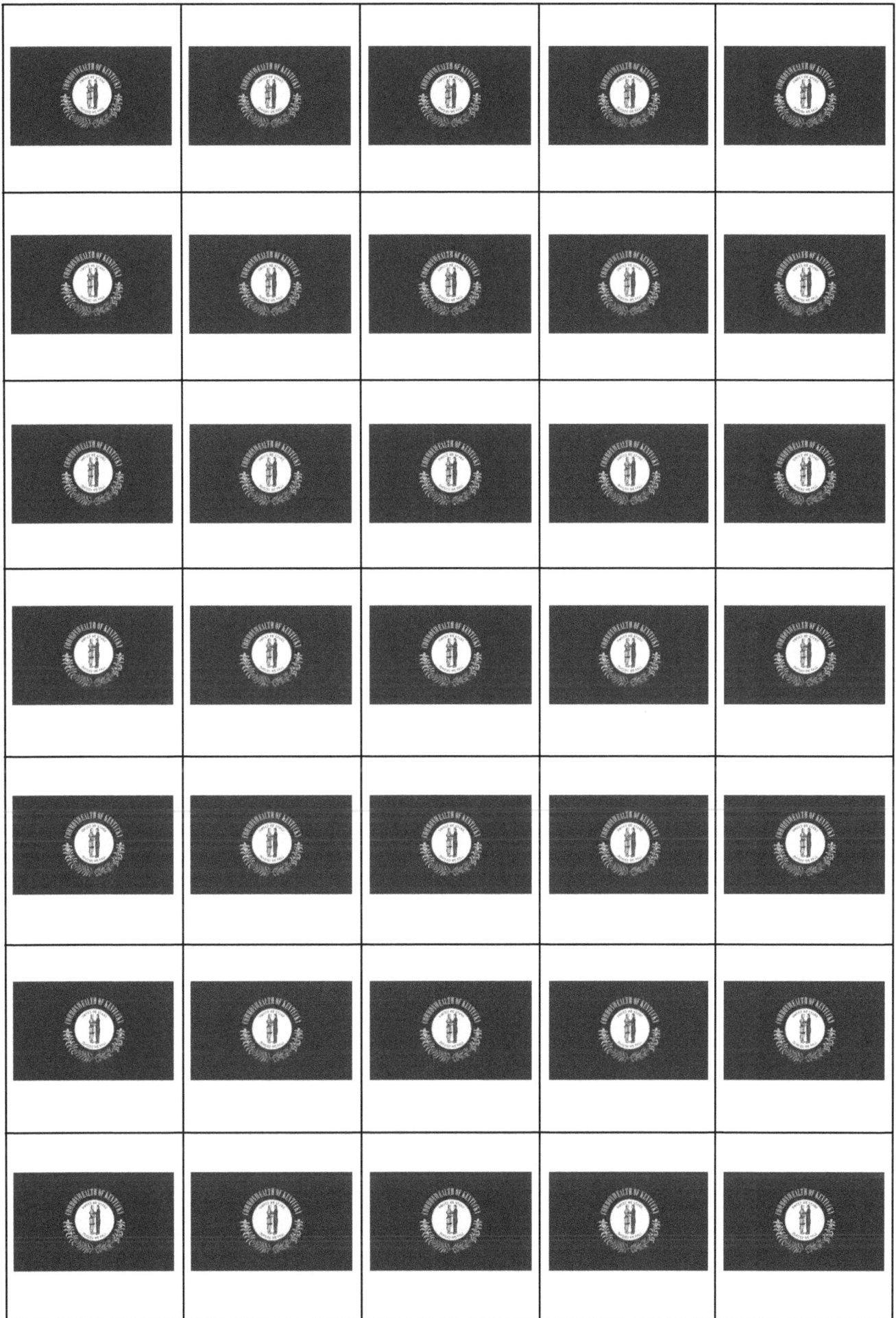

Muhammad Ali 1. This champion boxer was born in Louisville on January 17, 1942. He is nicknamed "The Greatest." 2. He won an Olympic gold medal for boxing in 1960.	**Appalachia** 1. ___ is a cultural region in the eastern United States. Eastern Kentucky is included in this region. 2. The Appalachian Mountains stretch from Belle Isle in Canada to Cheaha Mountain in Alabama; however, ___ usually refers only to the central and southern portions of the range.
Arboretum 1. I. W. Bernheim, a German immigrant, had a successful whiskey-distilling business. He gave Bernheim ___ and Research Forest to the people of Kentucky as a gift. 2. An ___ is place where trees and shrubs are cultivated for scientific and educational purposes.	**Black Mountain** 1. The highest point in Kentucky is ___ at 4,139 feet above sea level. It is in Harlan County. 2. ___ is one of the highest mountains in the Appalachia outside the Blue Ridge Mountains region.
Bluegrass 1. The ___ region is in the north-central part of Kentucky. Rolling meadows are surrounded by sandstone "knobs" on the east, south, and west. 2. The Knobs region is a narrow, horseshoe-shaped area of 100s of isolated hills. It wraps around the ___ Region in the center of the state.	**Daniel Boone** 1. This exploits of this pioneer, explorer, and frontiersman made him one of the first folk heroes of the United States. 2. ___ is most famous for his exploration and settlement of what is now Kentucky, but was then part of the unsettled area of Virginia.
Bordered 1. Kentucky is ___ by Illinois, Indiana, Ohio, Tennessee, West Virginia, Virginia, and Missouri. 2. Kentucky is ___ on the north by the Ohio River; it is ___ on the west by the Mississippi River.	**Cardinal(s)** 1. The ___ is the state. 2. Male ___ are a brilliant scarlet red; females are a buffy brown with reddish wings.
Christopher Carson 1. This frontiersman was nicknamed Kit. He was born in Madison County, Kentucky. 2. ___ was hired by John C. Fremont, who was known as the "Pathfinder," as a guide. He achieved national fame through Fremont's accounts of his expeditions.	**Civil War** 1. Kentucky was a border state during the ___. 2. Kentucky tried at first to stay neutral during the ___, but on September 7, 1861, it declared its allegiance to the Union.
Kentucky Bingo	© **Barbara M. Peller**

Climate
1. Kentucky has a moderate, relatively humid ___, with abundant rainfall.
2. The ___ in the southern and lowland regions is slightly warmer than the uplands.

Coal
1. The mining of ___ is an important industry in Kentucky.
2. ___ is the state mineral.

Commonwealth
1. The official name of the state of Kentucky is the ___ of Kentucky.
2. In this case, ___ means the same thing as "state."

County (-ies)
1. Kentucky is divided into 120 ___, which contain many incorporated cities.
2. Lexington and Fayette ___ and Louisville and Jefferson ___ have merged city-county governments.

Covered Bridge(s)
1. Kentucky has thirteen ___ still standing. Some are still in use.
2. Fleming County is called the ___ Capital of Kentucky.

Crop(s)
1. Tobacco, soybeans, corn for grain, and wheat are Kentucky's leading field ___.
2. Tobacco is the most important cash ___ in the state.

Cumberland Gap
1. The ___ was a pass through the Cumberland Mountains. It was an important part of the Wilderness Road.
2. The ___ is located just north of where present-day Kentucky, Tennessee and Virginia meet. Pioneers used this pass to go into the western frontiers of Kentucky and Tennessee.

Cumberland Plateau
1. The Appalachian Plateau is known as the ___ in Kentucky.
2. The ___ extends west to the Pottsville Escarpment and the eastern Knobs.

Cumberland River
1. Much of the ___ in and around Kentucky flows through and near the Daniel Boone National Forest.
2. Cumberland Falls is a large waterfall on the ___ in southeastern Kentucky. Under a full moon on clear nights, a moonbow is sometimes formed by the mist from the falls.

Jefferson Davis
1. ___, President of the Confederate States of America, was born in Kentucky.
2. Before he became President of the Confederacy, he was the 23rd secretary of war of the United States.

Kentucky Bingo

© Barbara M. Peller

Dulcimer 1. The Appalachian ___ is the state musical instrument. 2. The Appalachian ___ usually has 3 or 4 metal strings. The traditional way to play the ___ is to lay it flat on the lap. The player plucks the strings with the right hand while fretting with the left.	**Eastern Coal Field** 1. The ___ covers the eastern part of the state. The Cumberland Plateau is at the eastern end. Coal mining is the major industry in this region. 2. The ___ stretches from the Appalachian Mountains westward across the Cumberland Plateau to the Pottsville Escarpment.
Executive Branch 1. The ___ of state government comprises the governor, the lieutenant governor, the president of the Senate, the attorney general, and sometimes an auditor. 2. The governor is head of the ___ of state government. The present-day governor is [fill in].	**Flag** 1. The Kentucky ___ consists of the Seal of the Commonwealth on a field of navy blue. 2. A pledge of allegiance to the Kentucky ___ was adopted in 2000.
Frankfort 1. The capital of Kentucky is ___ in Franklin County. Kentucky State University is located here. 2. ___ is on the Kentucky River. Its name probably comes from Stephen Frank, a settler who was killed at what came to be known as Frank's Ford.	**Goldenrod** 1. ___ is the state flower. More than 30 varieties are native to Kentucky. 2. ___, the state flower is on the Great Seal, which is also on the state flag.
Hatfield–McCoy 1. The ___ feud lasted from 1863 to 1891. 2. The ___ feud involved two families of the West Virginia-Kentucky area in the Tug River Valley.	**Honeybee** 1. The ___ is the state agricultural insect. 2. The ___ is the official state symbol in 17 states, probably because it plays such an important role in agriculture.
Industry 1. The manufacture of transportation equipment is an important ___. 2. The manufacture of chemicals is also an important ___.	**Jackson Purchase** 1. The area known as ___ was purchased from the Chickasaw Indians by Andrew Jackson in 1818. 2. ___ is in the far western end of the state. It is in the Gulf Coastal Plain and has the lowest elevations in the state. It is bounded by the Mississippi and Ohio rivers and Kentucky Lake.

Kentucky Bingo

Judicial Branch
1. The ___ of state government comprises the Supreme Court, Court of Appeals, Circuit Court, Family Court, and District Court.
2. The ___ interprets what our laws mean and makes decisions about the laws and those who break them. The highest court of the ___ is the Supreme Court.

Kentucky Derby
1. The ___ is the 1st of 3 annual thorough-bred horse races that make up the Triple Crown. It is held annually in Louisville.
2. Churchill Downs hosts the annual Kentucky Derby on the first Saturday in May.

Kentucky Lake
1. ___ was formed by the creation of Kentucky Dam in the Tennessee River.
2. ___ is the largest manmade lake in the eastern United States. Other lakes in the state include Lake Barkley and Lake Cumberland.

Legislative Branch
1. The General Assembly, or ___ of state government, makes the laws.
2. The ___ of state government comprises the Senate and the House of Representatives.

Lexington
1. ___ is the second largest city in Kentucky. It is in the heart of the Bluegrass region of the state.
2. ___ is called "Thoroughbred City" and the "Horse Capital of the World."

Abraham Lincoln
1. ___ was born in a one-room log cabin on the Sinking Spring Farm in Hardin County, now LaRue County.
2. He became the 16th President of the United States.

Livestock
1. About 66% of the state's revenue from agriculture comes from ___ products.
2. Thoroughbred horses and beef cattle are Kentucky's most important ___ products.

Louisville
1. ___ is the largest city in the state. The ___ metropolitan area is sometimes called Kentuckiana because it includes counties in Southern Indiana.
2. The Kentucky Derby is held in ___.

Mammoth Cave
1. ___ is the world's longest known cave system. It is located in the northern part of the Pennyroyal region.
2. ___ is longer than the second- and third-longest cave systems combined.

Motto
1. *"Deo gratiam habeamus"* is the Commonwealth's official Latin ___.
2. In English the state ___ is "Let us be grateful to God."

Kentucky Bingo

Carrie Nation 1. ___ was a radical member of the temperance movement, which opposed alcohol. 2. This social reformer was born in Garrard County, Kentucky, on November 25, 1846.	**Native American(s)** 1. Most ___ were forced to leave Kentucky during the Indian Removals of the 1800s. 2. ___ who lived in what is now Kentucky included the Cherokee, the Chickasaw, the Shawnee, and the Yuchi tribes. There are no federally recognized Indian tribes in Kentucky today.
Ohio River 1. Kentucky cities along the ___ include Maysville, Ashland, Newport, Covington, Louisville, Owensboro, Henderson, and Paducah. 2. Tributaries of the ___ that flow in or through Kentucky include the Big Sandy, Cumberland, Green, Kentucky, Licking, and Tennessee rivers.	**Pearl(s)** 1. The freshwater ___ is the state gemstone. Freshwater ___ are found in many colors. Generally, they assume the color of the shell in which they form. 2. Freshwater ___ are formed in freshwater mussels; however, the population of freshwater mussels has been depleted.
Pennyroyal 1. The __ Region stretches west along the southern border of Kentucky from the Appalachian Plateau to Kentucky Lake. It features rolling hills and caves. 2. The ___ region is commonly called the Pennyrile. The center is a treeless area called the Barrens. The north features rocky ridges with underground caves and tunnels.	**Seal** 1. The Great ___ depicts two men clasping hands, one in buckskin and the other in more formal dress. 2. The outer ring of the Great ___ has the words "Commonwealth of Kentucky." The inner circle has the state motto, "United we stand. Divided we fall."
Song 1. "My Old Kentucky Home" is the state ___. 2. "Blue Moon Of Kentucky" is the state bluegrass ___.	**Union** 1. Kentucky was admitted to the ___ on June 1, 1792. Until then it was part of Virginia. 2. Kentucky was the 15th state to be admitted to the ___.
Western Coal Field 1. The ___ in the west-central part of the state is bordered on 3 sides by the Pennyroyal. The Ohio River is to the north. It is called the ___ because of its large coal deposits. 2. Not all of the counties in the ___ contain coal. Hopkins, Muhlenberg, and Ohio counties still have active mining. Kentucky Bingo	**Wilderness Road** 1. Daniel Boone blazed the ___ through the Cumberland Gap into central Kentucky. 2. The ___ was the principal route used by settlers for more than fifty years to reach Kentucky from the East. It was steep and rough and could only be crossed on foot or horseback.

Kentucky Bingo

Muhammad Ali	Appalachia	Arboretum	Bluegrass	County (-ies)
Cumberland Gap	Cumberland River	Eastern Coal Field	Frankfort	Honeybee
Industry	Jackson Purchase		Kentucky Derby	Legislative Branch
Lexington	Louisville	Motto	Carrie Nation	Ohio River
Pennyroyal	Seal	Song	Union	Western Coal Field

Kentucky Bingo

Pennyroyal	Seal	Flag	Louisville	Goldenrod
Judicial Branch	Covered Bridge(s)	Cardinal	Mammoth Cave	Kentucky Derby
Civil War	Eastern Coal Field		Executive Branch	Pearl(s)
Lexington	Abraham Lincoln	Honeybee	Western Coal Field	Bluegrass
Motto	Song	County (-ies)	Cumberland Gap	Native American(s)

Kentucky Bingo

Eastern Coal Field	Pearl(s)	Covered Bridge(s)	Hatfield–McCoy	Seal
Judicial Branch	Appalachia	Christopher Carson	Muhammad Ali	Dulcimer
Mammoth Cave	Song		Kentucky Derby	Black Mountain
Honeybee	Civil War	Kentucky Lake	Lexington	Flag
Native American(s)	Climate	County (-ies)	Western Coal Field	Goldenrod

Kentucky Bingo

Honeybee	Kentucky Derby	Arboretum	Climate	Goldenrod
Jackson Purchase	Bordered	Muhammad Ali	Louisville	Seal
Legislative Branch	Lexington		Stephen Collins Foster	Cumberland River
Pearl(s)	Appalachia	Song	County (-ies)	Cardinal
Coal	Motto	Daniel Boone	Native American(s)	Union

Kentucky Bingo: Card No. 4

Kentucky Bingo

Motto	Bluegrass	Mammoth Cave	Cardinal	Climate
Jackson Purchase	Pearl(s)	Christopher Carson	Executive Branch	Appalachia
Arboretum	Union		Industry	Jefferson Davis
Stephen Collins Foster	Goldenrod	Livestock	Western Coal Field	Commonwealth
Covered Bridge(s)	County (-ies)	Seal	Honeybee	Legislative Branch

Kentucky Bingo

Black Mountain	Kentucky Derby	Flag	Goldenrod	Union
Hatfield–McCoy	Mammoth Cave	Commonwealth	Seal	Muhammad Ali
Louisville	Coal		Bordered	Executive Branch
County (-ies)	Kentucky Lake	Western Coal Field	Daniel Boone	Arboretum
Judicial Branch	Cardinal	Livestock	Legislative Branch	Crop(s)

Kentucky Bingo

Livestock	Kentucky Derby	Jefferson Davis	Pearl(s)	Covered Bridge(s)
Judicial Branch	Goldenrod	Eastern Coal Field	Appalachia	Jackson Purchase
Union	Cumberland River		Executive Branch	Bordered
Honeybee	Lexington	Christopher Carson	Pennyroyal	Civil War
County (-ies)	Climate	Western Coal Field	Daniel Boone	Black Mountain

Kentucky Bingo

Legislative Branch	Kentucky Derby	Cumberland Plateau	Hatfield–McCoy	Bordered
Jackson Purchase	Arboretum	Louisville	Union	Cardinal
Crop(s)	Climate		Goldenrod	Bluegrass
Native American(s)	Honeybee	Pennyroyal	Coal	Lexington
Song	County (-ies)	Daniel Boone	Mammoth Cave	Judicial Branch

Kentucky Bingo: Card No. 8

Kentucky Bingo

Executive Branch	Covered Bridge(s)	Eastern Coal Field	Crop(s)	Climate
Coal	Goldenrod	Legislative Branch	Mammoth Cave	Kentucky Derby
Dulcimer	Livestock		Appalachia	Cumberland Plateau
Commonwealth	Bluegrass	Kentucky Lake	Industry	Jefferson Davis
Lexington	Western Coal Field	Christopher Carson	Pennyroyal	Stephen Collins Foster

Kentucky Bingo

Pennyroyal	Hatfield–McCoy	Bordered	Louisville	Crop(s)
Union	Cardinal	Muhammad Ali	Appalachia	Goldenrod
Climate	Kentucky Derby		Cumberland River	Civil War
Kentucky Lake	Stephen Collins Foster	Commonwealth	Western Coal Field	Dulcimer
Christopher Carson	Judicial Branch	Flag	Motto	Legislative Branch

Kentucky Bingo: Card No. 10

Kentucky Bingo

Black Mountain	Kentucky Derby	Mammoth Cave	Commonwealth	Judicial Branch
Cumberland Plateau	Dulcimer	Industry	Executive Branch	Muhammad Ali
Jackson Purchase	Goldenrod		Flag	Eastern Coal Field
Christopher Carson	Seal	Western Coal Field	Climate	Pennyroyal
Coal	County (-ies)	Livestock	Daniel Boone	Covered Bridge(s)

Kentucky Bingo: Card No. 11

Kentucky Bingo

Covered Bridge(s)	Bluegrass	Dulcimer	Hatfield–McCoy	Executive Branch
Eastern Coal Field	Judicial Branch	Arboretum	Daniel Boone	Appalachia
Livestock	Jefferson Davis		Union	Louisville
County (-ies)	Lexington	Goldenrod	Pennyroyal	Jackson Purchase
Kentucky Derby	Cumberland Plateau	Climate	Coal	Cardinal

Kentucky Bingo

Commonwealth	Bluegrass	Black Mountain	Dulcimer	Union
Arboretum	Cumberland Plateau	Goldenrod	Executive Branch	Civil War
Hatfield–McCoy	Cardinal		Eastern Coal Field	Jefferson Davis
Legislative Branch	Western Coal Field	Bordered	Climate	Pennyroyal
County (-ies)	Stephen Collins Foster	Daniel Boone	Livestock	Industry

Kentucky Bingo: Card No. 13

Kentucky Bingo

Cumberland Gap	Goldenrod	Mammoth Cave	Executive Branch	Coal
Cardinal	Livestock	Dulcimer	Appalachia	Kentucky Derby
Commonwealth	Cumberland River		Flag	Christopher Carson
Stephen Collins Foster	Western Coal Field	Climate	Bordered	Black Mountain
County (-ies)	Louisville	Civil War	Judicial Branch	Legislative Branch

Kentucky Bingo

Industry	Executive Branch	Mammoth Cave	Covered Bridge(s)	Hatfield–McCoy
Black Mountain	Flag	Muhammad Ali	Arboretum	Coal
Union	Livestock		Seal	Kentucky Derby
County (-ies)	Dulcimer	Cumberland Plateau	Western Coal Field	Commonwealth
Judicial Branch	Lexington	Daniel Boone	Crop(s)	Eastern Coal Field

Kentucky Bingo

Bordered	Dulcimer	Cumberland Plateau	Crop(s)	Abraham Lincoln
Louisville	Civil War	Jefferson Davis	Jackson Purchase	Cumberland River
Commonwealth	Bluegrass		Union	Eastern Coal Field
Honeybee	Cardinal	County (-ies)	Industry	Pennyroyal
Coal	Ohio River	Daniel Boone	Lexington	Kentucky Derby

Kentucky Bingo

Christopher Carson	Carrie Nation	Frankfort	Dulcimer	Cumberland Gap
Industry	Coal	Western Coal Field	Cumberland River	Jefferson Davis
Executive Branch	Legislative Branch		Ohio River	Cumberland Plateau
Stephen Collins Foster	Judicial Branch	Pennyroyal	Mammoth Cave	Civil War
Kentucky Lake	Commonwealth	Covered Bridge(s)	Hatfield–McCoy	Bluegrass

Kentucky Bingo

Crop(s)	Climate	Cardinal	Commonwealth	Louisville
Kentucky Derby	Christopher Carson	Kentucky Lake	Union	Coal
Executive Branch	Civil War		Frankfort	Arboretum
Bluegrass	Muhammad Ali	Western Coal Field	Pennyroyal	Flag
Ohio River	Dulcimer	Mammoth Cave	Carrie Nation	Black Mountain

Kentucky Bingo

Union	Black Mountain	Dulcimer	Cumberland Plateau	Pennyroyal
Industry	Hatfield–McCoy	Kentucky Derby	Covered Bridge(s)	Cumberland River
Carrie Nation	Climate		Appalachia	Seal
Flag	Ohio River	Kentucky Lake	Lexington	Frankfort
Arboretum	Abraham Lincoln	Judicial Branch	Legislative Branch	Daniel Boone

Kentucky Bingo: Card No. 19

Kentucky Bingo

Cumberland Gap	Carrie Nation	Hatfield–McCoy	Dulcimer	Daniel Boone
Cardinal	Eastern Coal Field	Jackson Purchase	Kentucky Lake	Louisville
Bluegrass	Jefferson Davis		Honeybee	Muhammad Ali
Motto	Song	Native American(s)	Lexington	Ohio River
Pearl(s)	Legislative Branch	Abraham Lincoln	Pennyroyal	Frankfort

Kentucky Bingo: Card No. 20

Kentucky Bingo

Industry	Black Mountain	Jackson Purchase	Dulcimer	Motto
Bluegrass	Frankfort	Bordered	Cumberland Plateau	Livestock
Civil War	Judicial Branch		Carrie Nation	Mammoth Cave
Kentucky Lake	Covered Bridge(s)	Ohio River	Stephen Collins Foster	Legislative Branch
Honeybee	Abraham Lincoln	Daniel Boone	Christopher Carson	Lexington

Kentucky Bingo

Crop(s)	Flag	Frankfort	Arboretum	Commonwealth
Louisville	Hatfield–McCoy	Seal	Cumberland Plateau	Appalachia
Cardinal	Cumberland River		Livestock	Jefferson Davis
Ohio River	Stephen Collins Foster	Lexington	Muhammad Ali	Jackson Purchase
Abraham Lincoln	Christopher Carson	Carrie Nation	Civil War	Honeybee

Kentucky Bingo

Bordered	Carrie Nation	Covered Bridge(s)	Arboretum	Daniel Boone
Black Mountain	Cumberland Gap	Judicial Branch	Industry	Muhammad Ali
Flag	Commonwealth		Native American(s)	Livestock
Civil War	Abraham Lincoln	Ohio River	Christopher Carson	Lexington
Motto	Song	Legislative Branch	Kentucky Lake	Frankfort

Kentucky Bingo: Card No. 23

Kentucky Bingo

Bordered	Legislative Branch	Cumberland Gap	Carrie Nation	Cumberland Plateau
Frankfort	Daniel Boone	Jackson Purchase	Louisville	Livestock
Jefferson Davis	Crop(s)		Commonwealth	Civil War
Motto	Native American(s)	Ohio River	Christopher Carson	Bluegrass
Pearl(s)	Honeybee	Abraham Lincoln	Hatfield–McCoy	Song

Kentucky Bingo

Honeybee	Jackson Purchase	Carrie Nation	Mammoth Cave	Frankfort
Muhammad Ali	Bluegrass	Industry	Bordered	Appalachia
Stephen Collins Foster	Cumberland Plateau		Native American(s)	Ohio River
Seal	Motto	Song	Abraham Lincoln	Cumberland River
Daniel Boone	Cumberland Gap	Cardinal	Coal	Pearl(s)

Kentucky Bingo

Frankfort	Carrie Nation	Flag	Louisville	Crop(s)
Kentucky Lake	Hatfield–McCoy	Cumberland Plateau	Cumberland Gap	Bordered
Stephen Collins Foster	Native American(s)		Cumberland River	Honeybee
Christopher Carson	Arboretum	Motto	Abraham Lincoln	Ohio River
Jefferson Davis	Coal	Mammoth Cave	Song	Pearl(s)

Kentucky Bingo

Flag	Cardinal	Carrie Nation	Cumberland Gap	Eastern Coal Field
Motto	Native American(s)	Industry	Ohio River	Appalachia
Western Coal Field	Song		Abraham Lincoln	Honeybee
Crop(s)	Black Mountain	Jackson Purchase	Pearl(s)	Muhammad Ali
Coal	Cumberland River	Frankfort	Seal	Jefferson Davis

Kentucky Bingo

Flag	Cumberland Gap	Seal	Carrie Nation	Bordered
Eastern Coal Field	Frankfort	Native American(s)	Louisville	Cumberland River
Song	Civil War		Jefferson Davis	Kentucky Lake
Pennyroyal	Crop(s)	Judicial Branch	Abraham Lincoln	Ohio River
Arboretum	Executive Branch	Coal	Pearl(s)	Motto

Kentucky Bingo

Frankfort	Cumberland Gap	Crop(s)	Industry	Executive Branch
Lexington	Kentucky Lake	Jackson Purchase	Jefferson Davis	Seal
Stephen Collins Foster	Native American(s)		Appalachia	Carrie Nation
Eastern Coal Field	Motto	Goldenrod	Abraham Lincoln	Ohio River
Bordered	Cumberland Plateau	Pearl(s)	Black Mountain	Song

Kentucky Bingo: Card No. 29

Kentucky Bingo

Climate	Carrie Nation	Louisville	Executive Branch	Ohio River
Muhammad Ali	Cumberland Gap	Flag	Cumberland River	Appalachia
Stephen Collins Foster	Commonwealth		Jefferson Davis	Jackson Purchase
Pearl(s)	Black Mountain	Arboretum	Abraham Lincoln	Native American(s)
Motto	Union	Song	Frankfort	Seal

Kentucky Bingo: Card No. 30